AF251446

# Sufism and Wisdom

Other books in the Sufism Lecture Series:

*Sufism*

*Sufism and Knowledge*

*Sufism and Islam*

*Sufism and Peace*

# Sufism
### and
# Wisdom

*Molana Salaheddin Ali Nader Shah Angha*
*"Pir Oveyssi"*

University of Provence
*April 1, 1995*

M.T.O. SHAHMAGHSOUDI® PUBLICATIONS

 M.T.O. SHAHMAGHSOUDI® PUBLICATIONS 

Angha, Salaheddin Ali Nader Shah

# Sufism and Wisdom



Library of Congress Catalog Card Number: 95-077982
ISBN: 0-910735-95-6

First edition: 1996
Second edition: 1997

Printed in the U.S.A.

Published and distributed by M.T.O. Shahmaghsoudi
5225 Wisconsin Ave., N.W.  Suite #502
Washington, D.C.  20015
U.S.A.

website: http://mto.shahmaghsoudi.org

# Contents

Wherever the masculine gender is used, it is solely for the purpose of linguistic convenience. Since the intent of religion is for the spiritual elevation of each individual, we believe that religion addresses the soul, and the soul is not subject to gender classification.

# Introduction

*A* few years ago Hazrat Pir began one of his lectures by asking the audience these questions, "If there were only one in the world, and that one were you, what would be your name? Who would you be? Would you hate? Would you love?" Only an instant lapsed before he calmly asked, "If there were one, and that one had all the knowledge of the universe, and could respond to all your needs and all your wants, what would you do?" Then he said, Sufism is about this "ONE".

Hazrat Pir's method of teaching is definitely thought provoking, and his students say demanding and challenging. Some say he evokes the same system of learning as Socrates did with his students. Those who have interviewed him usually confess that they are totally disarmed by his questions, becoming engaged in an intense learning experience. True to his mission, Hazrat Pir never ceases to teach. His main goal is to show people how they may attain the true state of human dignity, peace and tranquility. His definition of the human being rises above social, cultural and psychological definitions.

Sophisticated communication systems have linked people worldwide, breaking down the "absolutes" that societies, communities and countries had defined and kept sacred for themselves. It is the age of relativity. While exposure to diversity has expanded people's vision of the world, it has also brought elements of insecurity and instability into the day-to-day life of many people. When standards collapse and values shift, where can we find the ultimate definition of our "self"?

Hazrat Pir says, "Each person is a complex and unique masterpiece." Most people, if not all, would like this statement to be true. But what prevents us from experiencing it? What must happen for us to even understand the magnitude of this statement? If we don't allow our imagination to quickly define it, package it and file it away, we could start on a powerful journey of self-realization, which would change the entire fabric of societies, human interactions and legal and social systems. This means moving through the multidimensional patterns of social conditionings that have structured our lives, formed our identities, personalities, self-worth, our perceptions of others and our value systems.

How can we put these aside? And if we should put them aside what would be the yardstick with which we could measure our achievements, our knowledge and our understanding of anything?

Hazrat Pir says, "You are the measure for everything." He is often heard saying, "You have everything that you need. All you need to do is to lift the boundaries you have created, then 'reality' will unveil." But if one wants to be this "unique masterpiece", how, realistically, does one "lift the boundaries?"

"Know thyself," wrote the philosopher Plato about integrity; because "an unexamined life is not worth living." From the time of the Greeks, Western philosophy has advocated self-knowledge — internal learning. Internal learning is at the heart of Islam. As the Holy Prophet Muhammad has said, "Whoever knows the true self knows God."

To begin at the beginning — know thyself. The "i", the individual, is a cherished concept, the acknowledged foundation upon which democracy is built. By transforming the "i", one can go a long way towards transforming the greater world in which the "i" lives. The belief in the perfectibility of the Self has strengthened the fiber of Western society and the collapse of this belief in the twentieth century has brought about alienation and uncertainty in modern societies. Untouched by today's social, economic and political shifts, Hazrat Pir represents a strong and clear voice,

reminding us of the urgency to know the true and stable "I".
In so doing, he reaffirms the human being's capacity to master the self.

One of the significant contributions of Hazrat Pir to
the reservoir of world knowledge is the idea that, because
the world has projected its divisions and boundaries onto
the vulnerable "i", one must create a process for achieving
mastery of mind. This is done by first removing these divisions and boundaries onto the "i" through an inner experience of religion that begins with spiritual integration and
ends with a complete metamorphosis. It is no coincidence
that two of the healthiest and strongest mystical minds of
the Catholic tradition — St. John of the Cross and St. Teresa
of Avila — learned much about their mystical journey from
Islam as it was received into the Spanish Moorish tradition.

Much can be learned from the way Hazrat Pir teaches. Ideally, a student should think: "I will commit myself not
to the idea but the process of mastering my own mind and if
enough of us do the same 'the world' will simultaneously
change because 'the world' is us." A simple way of stating a
complicated process, but it is a beginning.

This series of essays, scripts of lectures given by
Hazrat Pir discusses his teaching as it relates to the history
of Sufism, peace, wisdom, knowledge, healing, meditation,
love, prayer, balance, and alchemy. The author, Hazrat Pir
Molana Salaheddin Ali Nader Shah Angha, is the forty-

second master of Maktab Tarighat Oveyssi Shahmaghsoudi *(School of Islamic Sufism)*, a school that traces its lineage back to the very advent of Islam in the seventh century A.D. While Hazrat Pir's lectures are faithful to the tradition which produced him and which he now guides, they also reflect the mark he has made on that tradition. Raised and trained in the esoteric tradition of Sufism and educated in the West, Hazrat Pir is exceptionally sensitive to the modern world. Accomplished in the disciplines of religion, science, philosophy and poetry, and trained by his father, Molana Hazrat Shah Maghsoud Sadegh Angha (Professor Angha), himself a great master of Sufism and an advanced physicist, Hazrat Pir has, from a very young age developed not only a perceptive and accomplished mind, but also an expansive spirit.

Our desire to transform the world, he teaches, must begin with a transformation of "i" into "I", the true Self. To the Sufi, this necessitates a dialogue between heart and mind. What Westerners call internal learning, or self-knowledge is, to the Sufi, more like a glorified "i" short of a transformation into Self. For example, Hazrat Pir teaches that drug addiction, the scourge of modern society, will elude well-meaning people's attempts to eradicate it, until they understand how to heal the mind of its addiction, and discover the stable "I". To heal the mind of its addiction, one must acknowledge that God, and not the ego is at the center of the "I". Only then is one capable of living a healthy and balanced life.

A serious scrutiny of Hazrat Pir's example would serve the purpose of welcoming a science of mind that may well complement the existing one in the West. Islam is much in the news these days and concerned people want to know more about a culture that is at once alien and familiar — as familiar as the lines from the *Holy Qur'an,* "I am closer to you than your jugular vein." Most Westerners would not have ever read these words unless they were familiar with a poem of the same name by French writer James Sacré. Yet there is a certain basic sanity about those words rooted in a deeper source than that of the creative ego. Heirs of the Greek tradition, the West is only beginning to realize why the heart of Islam seems so close — it has always been there, part of its world, part of its culture, part of its "I" from the beginning.

So it seems fitting that on American soil, a nation founded on the spirit of exploration and discovery, Hazrat Pir has designed and built a memorial in memory of his teacher and father, Professor Angha. In three dimensions, near Novato, California stands a wonderful metaphor for 1400 years of spiritual labor and the integration of the human being's consciousness. There in architecture and here in words on the page, Hazrat Pir encourages the seeker to submit to his or her own metamorphosis and flower like the art of the memorial through the integration of Self, through integrity to the final union with God.

# Sufism
### and
# Wisdom

*In the Name of God*
*Most Gracious, Most Merciful*

*Praise be to God, the summit of perfection and knowledge, the Eternal, the Gracious. He exists, but not by accident, and His existence is not contingent upon anything; He exists, but not from nonexistence. He is with everything, but not in parallel with anything; and He is other than anything but is not separate; He destined the powers and the forces and the heavens, from which He made the seven skies in harmony and balance; within them He placed the sun, the moon, and the stars in their constellations; and everything in the universe, in surrender, forever pulsates to the call of Existence. The night was deemed for knowledge of Him, and the day for the light of His effusions. God's grace be upon His chosen and praised Messenger, Muhammad Mostafa, and his pure and innocent followers and successors.*

Wisdom and knowledge are words that evoke a sense of inspiration and aspiration, and perhaps awe, in most people. When aligned with Sufism, they become more compelling and to a great extent mystified. But what do these words really mean? I believe that it is important to demystify things, for them to become accessible and applicable so that all of us may benefit from them, for "the wise attracts benefit and repels loss".[1] I believe this to be the essential function of knowledge.

Having been trained in the discipline of Sufism since childhood, under the guidance of my grandfather and father, the fortieth and the forty-first Masters of Maktab Tarighat Oveyssi Shahmaghsoudi, I have learned that the true scholar is not satisfied with the result of other people's findings, but makes every effort to discover truth for himself. The human quest for knowledge is only valid when its goal is to discover the reality behind the surface value of words, things, entities, etc.

If we take a quick look at the evolutionary process of the various disciplines, we will see that through several thousand years of history, from one single branch called wisdom, thousands of branches have evolved under the headings of science and humanities. If we take a closer look, we will see that the cause of this expansion has been the inquisitive spirit of the human being with its unquenchable thirst to know — an innate drive that doesn't cease to motivate. This urge to know is innate to each human being, irrespective of race, gender, color, religion, etc.

The function of knowledge is to expand, to illuminate, to present, and so forth. The seed bursts open from its shell in order to manifest its knowledge by presenting its roots, stem, leaves, flower and fruit. The sun shines unceasingly, the elements come together and disperse, and come together and disperse. With each gathering and dispersion, a new manifestation of knowledge is witnessed. Can you point to anything that is not the manifestation of knowledge? Knowledge is absolute!

The human quest for knowledge begins at birth. In reality, it is an urge to return to the Origin — Knowledge. As I continue speaking, hopefully the meaning of what I have just said will become clear for you. When a child is born, his mental screen is clear. He is born with infinite capabilities and possibilities. From the moment of birth, the infant begins to expand his domain of experience. The fetus in the womb has hands, has eyes, has ears, has all the organs, but does not use them. He has no idea what the sense of touch or taste is like. He has no idea about the visual images he will be encountering, nor the sounds he will be hearing. It doesn't take long before his urge to know prompts him to explore his environment and use the various tools that his innate knowledge had made possible for him during the various phases of growth as a fetus.

As he interacts with his environment, the clear screen of his mind begins to be imprinted with various experiences, forming a back up system with which he begins to assess new incoming information. He then begins to recognize familiar sounds, voices, objects, tastes, etc. As the data increases in the memory files of the brain, more cross references are needed to identify and classify new information, so repeatedly registered information becomes more reinforced and more accessible. Thus, various habits, behavior and thought patterns are formed.

All incoming new information is either accepted or rejected, depending upon whether or not it is in harmony with what already exists. Parents want to give their children what benefits them and makes them comfortable. They want to protect their children from harm. They want to pass on their experiences, feelings, and thoughts to their children —all of which have either been handed down to them by their own parents, or shaped and reshaped by their society, culture and environment — even those concerning religion and God. While one's thoughts may contain some kind of truth, what one receives from the verbal word, or what I call a symbol or contract, does not contain its meaning, even if it creates imaginary references to what it should be.

Now, if I were to come and tell you about God, and what I told you did not cross-reference with the image you have in your mind of God, you would either say, "He's crazy", or "He doesn't know." Whereas, if the words that I spoke about God had formed an image in your mind early on, that would be the basis for the measurement of new information. In either case, the information you have collected is invalid and void of knowledge. If you look closely, you will see that your understanding of God was based on what others had described to you, and not your own experience. You had merely accepted what others had said.

The above example can be applied to all unknowns for people. Examples are heaven, hell, eternity, infinity, angel, demons, etc. The meaning of these words are with those who spoke about them, and not with those who blindly repeat them and form images of them in their minds. It is explicitly stated in the *Holy Qur'an (17:36)*, "Pursue not that of which you have no knowledge."

How do we distinguish between knowledge, imagination, and illusion? Knowledge is that which we gain through our own personal experience, whereas, illusion is merely giving shape and form to things and events in our minds that have not been our personal experience. Let me clarify that the word experience does not mean repetition. To repeat one thing over and over, does not create an experience, it simply reinforces our imagination of that word, whatever that word may be. As an example, I have a dog, and let's say I call him Sam. The word "Sam" has no meaning nor symbolic reference for the dog, but over a period of time, because I keep repeating the name Sam, he will respond. What is he responding to? He is responding to the sound and the tone of my voice, all of which are within the word Sam. This is a contract and not an understanding, nor an experience. Experience is another word for the actualization of knowledge in every aspect of life. It is not an entity that is variable and cannot be accessed and used in time of need.

People think that if they read or hear about things, they also know them. For example, you know what love is, if you have experienced it; you know what sadness is if you have experienced it; you know what joy is if you have experienced it. No matter how much effort I exert in explaining any of the above feelings to you, you will not know what I am talking about unless you have experienced it. Perhaps, you can imagine what I am trying to convey, but the experience of those feelings are not yours. Therefore, those words have no reality for you. We must not forget that, "Words cannot transfer the meaning."[2]

Do you know why there are so many "religions", sects, belief systems, etc.? It is because people's knowledge of God is no more than imagination and illusion. If you and I are both precious gem experts, would we dispute whether or not a pearl is a pearl or a diamond a diamond? Of course not, we would immediately recognize a diamond to be a diamond and not a sapphire or ruby, or whatever else. Would two children who have been reared by the same parents fight with each other about who their parents are? The answer is obvious. Can we assume that the reason for so much religious disputes, hatreds and wars is that God is missing from people's experience?

People think that by reading books, listening to lectures, or following someone blindly, they will know God. If you memorize with total accuracy all the writings of Einstein, will you have his knowledge? Or, if you memorize his formula $E = mc^2$, will you have the knowledge that the formula represents, or, if you repeat the formula thousands of times, will you gain access to that knowledge? Or, if I am an excellent writer and scholar, but have no knowledge of physics, and I write a detailed account of the life and works of Einstein, will you think that I have the same knowledge as he?

In physical, tangible matters we do not make such assumptions. If we did, we would be either fired, retired, or put away. But, when it comes to issues relating to God, and the message of God, only assumption and illusion are the basis of our understanding. This is why so much superstition surrounds all religious practices. Blind faith is handed down generation after generation, taking the color of the environment, culture, geographical and ethnic conditions of people. Religion has become no more than a commodity, transacted for various purposes and goals.

But what is the essence of the teachings of the Prophets, how is it related to Sufism, and what is its relevance for today? If we look objectively and with sincerity at the lives and teachings of the Holy Prophets, it will be very clear that their lives were devoted to announcing, and sharing with others, their unique discovery. The method through which they had arrived at their discovery was not because of what others had said before them, nor because they feared or trusted someone. Instead, they had an innate unquenchable urge to "know" which could not be satisfied except through personal experience.

Like the Prophets, true scientists devote their life to study and research, and whenever they make a discovery, they see it as their duty to announce it for the benefit and welfare of humanity. They do not force others to accept, nor do they ask people to accept blindly what they have said. They invite the scientific community to go through the same process of research and discovery as they had, so they may also arrive at the same results. The Prophets have always said, validate what we are saying through your own experience, so you may discover the truth for yourself.

Hazrat Shah Maghsoud Sadegh Angha, in his book *Dawn*, has explained this very clearly. He states that the Prophets appeared at a time when people were worshipping idols. The Prophets told the people that the idols they had created with their own hands were limited, and not worthy of worship. They told them that they knew God, they were in communication with God, and that what they told them were His words. They said, God had given these directions, so they might act on these words, and know Him, and not worship idols.[3]

What people did and still do, is take the words of the Prophets and cross reference them with what exists in their memory files, and imagine God accordingly. Is this the God the Prophets were speaking about? Is this god great, and worthy of worship? Is it not less worthy than the idols of the past?

The essence of the message of the Prophets is that each person must individually cognize God in his or her being. God cannot be known through what He has said, or what others say. This is philosophy — unvalidated knowledge —

whereas, the knowledge of the Prophets is validated through personal experience or absolute cognition.

We never accept that a child has knowledge of medicine because his parents are physicians, but we say we are Moslems, Jews, Christians, etc. because we were born into a family who are Moslems, Jews, or Christians. Isn't this absurd? How can we justify such ignorance? Can you inherit such knowledge genetically, or environmentally?

Knowledge of the Prophets is the knowledge of absolute existence, therefore it is vast and eternal. Whereas, knowledge acquired through sensory perception registered and processed in the brain is limited. The brain functions much like a computer. It works according to the program it is given, and cannot go beyond that. Its input frequency and output response change with the addition of new information. The brain is the organizer, the manager, and the commander of the body. Its function is to operate this machinery to its optimum capacity and protect it from danger. Its mode of operation doesn't exceed this. It is nurtured by nature, and it interacts with nature. The realm of nature is forever changing and nothing is constant. The cycles of nature, the evolutionary changes of living organisms, or the life cycles of beings, are evident examples of this.

If we were to agree on the definition of truth as being that which "exists and is constant,"[4] then we would realize the significance of the message of the Prophets. The

infinite cannot be known through the limited — the senses
and the brain are limited.

One of the basic principles of Sufism is that you cannot know anything that is outside of you, because to know
something in its totality requires that you be that entity.
Since our recognition of things is based on contracts and our
understanding of those symbols, and because our feelings
keep shifting and our senses are continuously activated, we
cannot know anything outside of ourselves. Therefore, the
best place to look for the answers to our being is right within the unbounded reality of ourselves. In this context, each
person is the researcher, the laboratory, and the subject of
study.

Perhaps if I explain the different levels of the human
being, you will more readily understand what I have just
said. The human being consists of the following four levels:

The outermost level is the level of nature, which is
the laboratory for human experience.

The second level is the physiological level, the cellular, organic level which functions according to its own
inherent programs and laws. The activities of this level are
generally a combination of sensory activities, thought, cellular needs, and experiences, as well as cultural heritage
and personal aptitudes. Medical science focuses on this
level and its useful technological and treatment advances
have dealt with aspects of the cellular, organic level.

The third level is the developmental level, the locus for mental, sensory and psychic powers and for the development and interrelationship of the magnetic bodies.

The fourth level is the innermost level, the mysterious level, which is the point of stability and true personality. Amir al-Mo'menin Ali (peace be upon him) said, "Do you think you are an insignificant germ? The greater world lies within you." This is the level which is the source of knowledge as announced by the Prophets, and the focus of the teachings of Maktab Tarighat Oveyssi Shahmaghsoudi.

Each level of the human being has its own sphere of operation and is submitted to the laws governing it. The instructions of the Prophets are meant to acquaint people with all the levels of their being, their interaction and relationship with the extensive universe, and the laws governing their being, so they may live in peace and tranquility and know their eternity.

The Holy Prophet Muhammad has said, "Knowledge is not obtained through scholarship, but it is a light that God shines in the heart of whom He wills." As mentioned earlier, the function of knowledge is to dispel ignorance and illuminate the darkness.

The Prophets, Saints, and the Enlightened have always shared with the people of their time the ways and means of how they attained their wisdom and knowledge. They have said that humans are ignorant of their true identity and their true human right. They have said that humans live in darkness. Their definition of the human being far exceeds those provided by various theoretical and scientific disciplines. They see humans caged in the boundaries of limitation that they themselves have created. The Prophets see humans in such a way. They see humans burdened and anchored to limitation because of their attachments, needs, prejudices, biases, etc.

The materialistic attachments, and their influence, create solid boundaries for people in which they become trapped — prisoners of ignorance and self-inflicted bondage. The essential message of the Prophet is that: You are created free. Know your true dignity and your eternity. However, the identity people formulate for themselves is based on what their society, family, culture and country provide for them, which they unconsciously obey, without knowledge.

People's basis for measuring who they are and their self-worth are these changeable social and cultural factors. In contrast, the Prophet Muhammad (peace and blessings upon him) has said, "Whoever cognizes the true self, has cognized God."

In Islam, the dignity assigned to the true personality of humans is no other than the Divine. Sufism is a discipline, a method and a way that teaches humans how to attain their true state of dignity as stated by the Prophets. Therefore, Sufism is the reality of religion. Sufism is the method through which the Prophets attained the cognition of God, and their true self and personality.

The accurate word for Sufism is *irfan*, derived from the Arabic word *ma'rifa*, meaning to cognize, to know. When can we say we know something? When nothing about the subject of inquiry remains unknown to us. Perhaps, the best way to describe Sufism is to say, it is the School of Self-Knowledge. It teaches its students to discover their hidden talents and abilities; expand their perception; break the boundaries of limitation; and ultimately journey through the heavens of their being.

My father, Hazrat Shah Maghsoud Sadegh Angha, Pir Oveyssi, in his book, *The Principles of Faghr and Sufism*, has said that the human being is not a mass of cells, but an intricate weave of the heavens and the earth in whom lies all potential — from the beast to that surpassing the angels, from darkness to light. In essence, the human being has a choice as to where and what he wants to be in this intricate and infinite fabric of Existence. He has further said, "When nature wanted to manifest itself in its most subtle of forms, it became an entity called the human being."[5]

Just as the physical sciences have endeavored to know the physical aspects of the human being, the social scientists have endeavored to know his motivations, and the reasons for his behaviors and actions. With all the sophisticated research, the human being still remains a mystery to them. Essentially, all of their efforts are geared towards facilitating human life on earth, by making advances in technology and agriculture, and by manipulating nature and the genetic codes.

What remains hidden from their sphere of study is the "I" who is the doer behind all investigation, search, and action. Who is the "I" that does not cease to voice its presence from the moment of birth, and remains constant throughout life, although everything else goes through the cycle of change? Islam gives such a high rank to the human being, that it leaves no separation between "I" and God. This is the wisdom and knowledge of the Prophets.

The way to self-knowledge begins with an innate urge on the part of the seeker who genuinely wants to know the reason for his being, becoming and the hereafter. In other words, he finds himself between two unknowns — where he came from, and where he will go. He is seeking answers that are not available through the investigative and theoretical disciplines.

The Prophet of Islam has said, "I am the city of Knowledge, and Ali is its door." Entering the realm of God requires the presence of a teacher who has been inwardly introduced to the seeker by God. In the *Holy Qur'an (57:9)* it is stated, "He is the One Who sends to His servant manifest Signs, that He may lead you from the depths of darkness into the Light." And, *(57:17)* "Already have We shown the Signs plainly to you, that ye may learn wisdom."

To attain the state of wisdom and knowledge, the seeker must go through the seven states of transformation and purification under the guidance of the *Pir* (Spiritual Teacher), who has been inwardly revealed by God. The seven states reflect the process through which the seeker (*salik*) begins to move from the external to the internal; from a state of dependency on the external to a state of inward stability; from a state of agitation to a state of tranquility; from a state of being needy to a state of fulfillment; from a state of limitation to a state of discovery and expansion.

These states reflect the changes that take place. For example, being in control of all natural appetites, desires, and dependencies (emotional, physical, etc.), the seeker begins to feel an inward release and a sense of freedom and peace. The constant external attractions that had pulled him in different directions no longer control him.

As the seeker puts into practice the instructions he has received from the *Pir* — prayers, fasting, meditation, and *zikr* (remembrance of God) — the realm of the heart and soul become accessible to him. He begins the journey to the hidden and mysterious realm of his being. It is during these times of spiritual elevation that the seeker transcends the boundaries of time and place and enters the state of witnessing and cognition which are inaccessible to the senses.

The seeker's ultimate goal is to dissolve in the Absolute Truth — God. The directions and instructions he receives from the *Pir* are to guide him to reach the stage of cognition as stated in the *Holy Qur'an (24:37)*, "Men whom neither traffic nor merchandise can divert from the remembrance of God, nor from regular Prayer". Bayazid Bastami, a disciple of Imam Ja'far Sadegh (peace be upon him) has said, "No other but God is within my robe."[6]

As you can see from the above, Sufism is a discipline, a system of education that transforms humans from their base state, to their divine state. Each of the stages brings with it a change, a revolution and evolution for the seeker.

During this process of transformation and training, the seeker's awareness expands as he develops the subtle dimensions hidden within him. For example, one of the keys to progress toward this realization is *zikr* (remembrance). The formal rendition of *zikr* is in prayer and in chants. Both include the *zikr* of words, *zikr* of movement of the body, and *zikr* of heart. It is a process of purification of the heart, of cleansing and releasing. In the stages of *zikr*, first all is relinquished, then he who is witnessing the Presence forgets the *zikr*, and thirdly, he shall no longer see himself, but only the Divine Beloved, "All that is on earth will perish: But will abide (for ever) the Face of thy Lord." (*Holy Qur'an, 55:26,27*).

My grandfather, Hazrat Mir Ghotbeddin Mohammad Angha, in his book, *From Fetus to Paradise: The Evolutionary States of Man* has said:

> Bird of paradise I am,
> To this earth I belong not.
> This body's been made a cage
> Just for a few brief days.[7]

There are many layers connecting the physical body to the spiritual realm. These levels are directly connected to the electromagnetic centers existing in different locations in the human being, each serving a specific function as well as working in a continuous relationship with the various organs and glands. There are thirteen main electromagnetic centers and numerous minor ones. The main center is located in the heart, and has been called by my father ***the source of life in the heart***.[8] This center is very important in the teachings of the *School of Islamic Sufism*. Amir al-Mo'menin Ali (peace be upon him) has said, "The heart is an open book."

The return to the origin, of which I spoke earlier, refers to this center in the heart. A brief period after conception (twenty-one days), a pulsation occurs in the mass of cells, and from this point the heart begins to form. After the heart is formed, the nerves begin to branch out and ultimately the brain and the other parts evolve.

The heart is the seat of knowledge in the teachings of Sufism. This is why meditation in the heart is so crucial and important. It is returning to the source of our being, the source of knowledge and our true identity.

The first layer beyond the physical body which the seeker becomes familiar with, is the etheric body. This is the template or mold for the physical body. This spiritual body has a spiritual heart which is hidden behind the physical heart. The "secret or hidden heart", as it is known in the Sufi tradition, is directly connected with the existential healing powers. The spiritual heart transmits spiritual energy which forms a body embracing the physical body. This etheric or corporeal body is adapted to the palpable world. It is the origin of the body's electrical current, which is transmitted from the spiritual heart to the physical heart. Disconnection of this power from the heart will cause the heart to stop beating. The etheric body vanishes two or three days after the soul separates from the body.

The second body is the celestial or astral body. This body is more tender, and is situated over the etheric body. It originates in the heavenly celestial world and is the communication link with the spiritual world.

The third body is the rational body. It is more delicate, luminous and transparent than the celestial body. Revelation and inspiration originate from this body. The souls of Prophets, Saints and the Enlightened guide seekers to the celestial sphere through this body. They also inspire luminous thoughts and divine ideas in the hearts of truth seekers.

The fourth body is the luminous body, sometimes called the fire halo. This body is responsible for the ascension of the rational soul to the spiritual world. The soul of man can only attain this position through great patience and devotion. Those souls who sacrifice themselves to serve others with a fervent love, will form a luminous halo, similar to the halo around the moon. This is the luminous halo painted around the heads of the Prophets and Saints.

Any true system of education is supposed to dispel ignorance. The principles of Sufism, based on the pillars of Islam, are a set of instructions intended for the serious student who wishes to discover his or her reality, which result in freedom, stability and knowledge. These results cannot be attained through blind faith, rituals, trust, hallucination, repetition, or whatever is handed down from parents, society, and culture. Unfortunately, as in all "religious practices", it is not uncommon to see the teachings of Sufism reduced to no more than ritualistic practices appealing to the imagination of people, void of reality. The Prophet Mohammad (peace and blessings upon him) has said, "Faith is not achieved for the asking, but settles in the heart and is confirmed by actions."

Would anyone who has undergone the training and transformation described above, steal, murder, hate, hoard, kill, rape, or abuse? The answer is evident. If we separate the prevalent religious teachings and practices from the essence of the message of the Prophets it will be clear why religion has lost its dignity and value in the lives of people. Unless human nature is transformed, unless people become acquainted with, and begin to experience their more subtle and tender levels of being, societies will not change, and aggression, hatred, and killings will continue to devastate human lives.

Religion in its true sense is not only for the benefit of the individual, but also for the health and welfare of society, as well as stability in nature.

I have endeavored today, to present to you to the greatest extent possible, the knowledge underlying the message of the Prophets, whose reality is presented and taught in the School of Islamic Sufism — the School of Self-Knowledge. Perhaps those who are susceptible of heart and mind have heard my words, and will act upon them to bridge the alienation that has evolved through the ages between religion and knowledge. Perhaps, those of you who are receptive, will want to explore and discover the reality of your own being, to find out for yourself the truth of the message of the Prophets.

If my words have touched one single soul today I know I will have done my duty as ordained by the Lord of believers, the God of the heavens and earth.

May God grant you the wisdom of Socrates, so you may confess your ignorance before the infinite Existence.

May He grant you the gifts he bestowed upon His chosen: abstention from Abraham, remembrance from Moses, fasting from Jesus, annihilation and subsistence in God from Mohammad, and a thirst with which you will endeavor on the path of Self-Knowledge, excavating the treasures of your being and reaping their benefits for the health, happiness, and prosperity of yourself, your family, society, country, and the world.

The Holy Prophet Mohammad (peace and blessings upon him) has said, "The human being is like a mine — gold, silver, or jewel — excavate their goodness, so you may have peace."

# Endnotes


1. Angha, Hazrat Shah Maghsoud Sadegh. (1989). *Dawn*. Lanham, MD: University Press of America, p. 25

2. *Dawn*. p. 30

3. *Dawn*. pp. 17-18.

4. *Dawn*. p. 25.

5. Angha, Hazrat Shah Maghsoud Sadegh. *The Principles of Faghr & Sufism*. (1987). Verdugo City, CA: M.T.O. Shahmaghsoudi Publications. p. 10.

6. Angha, Hazrat Shah Maghsoud Sadegh. (1986). *Al-Rasa'el*. Lanham, MD: University Press of America. p. 19

7. Angha, Hazrat Mir Ghotbeddin Mohammad. (1987). *Az Janin ta Janan (From Fetus to Paradise: The Evolutionary States of Man)*. Verdugo City, CA: M.T.O. Shahmaghsoudi® Publications. p. 22.

8. Angha, Hazrat Shah Maghsoud Sadegh. (1986). *The Mystery of Humanity: Tranquility and Survival*. Lanham, MD: University Press of America.

# Genealogy of Maktab Tarighat Oveyssi Shahmaghsoudi
## (School of Islamic Sufism)®

**Prophet Mohammad**
**Imam Ali**
Hazrat Oveys Gharani*
Hazrat Salman Farsi
Hazrat Habib-ibn Salim Ra'i
Hazrat Soltan Ebrahim Adham
Hazrat Abu Ali Shaqiq al-Balkhi
Hazrat Sheikh Abu Torab Nakhshabi
Hazrat Sheikh Abi Amr al-Istakhri
Hazrat Abu Ja'far Hazza
Hazrat Sheikh Kabir Abu Abdollah Mohammad-ibn Khafif Shirazi
Hazrat Sheikh Hossein Akkar
Hazrat Sheikh Morshed Abu-Isshaq Shahriar Kazerouni
Hazrat Khatib Abolfath Abdolkarim
Hazrat Ali-ibn Hassan Basri
Hazrat Serajeddin Abolfath Mahmoud-ibn Mahmoudi Sabouni Beyzavi
Hazrat Sheikh Abu Abdollah Rouzbehan Baghli Shirazi
Hazrat Sheikh Najmeddin Tamat-al Kobra Khivaghi
Hazrat Sheikh Ali Lala Ghaznavi
Hazrat Sheikh Ahmad Zaker Jowzeghani
Hazrat Noureddin Abdolrahman Esfarayeni
Hazrat Sheikh Alaoddowleh Semnani
Hazrat Mahmoud Mazdaghani
Hazrat Amir Seyyed Ali Hamedani
Hazrat Sheikh Ahmad Khatlani
Hazrat Seyyed Mohammad Abdollah Ghatifi al-Hasavi Nourbakhsh
Hazrat Shah Ghassem Feyzbakhsh
Hazrat Hossein Abarghoui Janbakhsh
Hazrat Darvish Malek Ali Joveyni
Hazrat Darvish Ali Sodeyri
Hazrat Darvish Kamaleddin Sodeyri
Hazrat Darvish Mohammad Mozaheb Karandehi (Pir Palandouz)
Hazrat Mir Mohammad Mo'men Sodeyri Sabzevari
Hazrat Mir Mohammad Taghi Shahi Mashhadi
Hazrat Mir Mozaffar Ali
Hazrat Mir Mohammad Ali
Hazrat Seyyed Shamseddin Mohammad
Hazrat Seyyed Abdolvahab Naini
Hazrat Haj Mohammad Hassan Kouzekanani
Hazrat Agha Abdolghader Jahromi
Hazrat Jalaleddin Ali Mir Abolfazl Angha
Hazrat Mir Ghotbeddin Mohammad Angha
Hazrat Molana Shah Maghsoud Sadegh Angha
Hazrat Salaheddin Ali Nader Shah Angha

*The conventional Arabic transliteration is Uways al-Qarani*